John David Rees

Notes of a Journey from Kasveen to Hamadan Across the Karagan Country

John David Rees

Notes of a Journey from Kasveen to Hamadan Across the Karagan Country

ISBN/EAN: 9783744694650

Printed in Europe, USA, Canada, Australia, Japan

Cover: Foto ©Andreas Hilbeck / pixelio.de

More available books at **www.hansebooks.com**

summer retreat of the Kings of Media and Persia. Hamadan itself has been fully described. Kasveen is known to every traveller from Teheran to Resht *en route* for Europe, but the intervening country is unknown to Europeans, so far as I could learn after the fullest inquiry at Teheran and elsewhere. An Austrian botanist (Dr. Pulak) had once gone *viâ* Ab-i-garm and Kabouterkhana to Hamadan, but this left a large tract of hill and plain, due south of Kasveen and due east of the places mentioned, untouched.

Most travellers in Persia have inferred I think, or have given their readers the impression that they have inferred, that the country they have passed through is a fair sample of the country as a whole, and the travellers who have been off the postal route from Bushire to Teheran and Resht are few. Now, that route skirts the east of the great desert and is, in fact, at least as sterile, except where it passes through the plains of Shiraz, Kazeroon, and Ispahan, as any part of Persia, the desert proper alone excluded. True it is known that the Bakhtiari country and parts of Luristan present a very different appearance. Major Bell and Mr. Stack are the latest witnesses on this point. Again the beaten track from Teheran to Hamadan, and thence to the Turkish frontier, has been fully described.

Is it known, however, that away up to the Elburz range extend fertile and well-watered plains covered with corn, and vineyards, and orchards, and hills, that, unirrigated, give a fair annual return of wheat—hills which did not fail to do this even in the disastrous famine of 1870 ? These notes will show that such is the character of the tract I traversed, while my inquiries go to show further that the other tract referred to, viz., that between Kom and Hamadan, much resembles it. Nor is the country south of this, about Sultanabad and Gulpaigan, less fertile, while further south again the country of the Karun and the Tigris is reached, a part of what was, till war and rapine destroyed it, the garden of the world.

It has happened that many writers have, from military and other considerations, chiefly confined their observations to the country bordering on Afghanistan and Beloochistan, while that west of the main route from sea to sea has received the attention for the most part of savants who were chiefly interested in its archæology.

At any rate it is the case, I venture to think, that the public at large, and many of the informed minority, do not appreciate in its full significance the fact that the whole country west of the beaten track, to the country to the east of it, and to the coast of the Persian Gulf. Not that the most barren regions of Persia that are inhabited do not well support the scanty population that dwells therein.

Again, if portions of the country are shown to be more fertile and populous than is commonly supposed, and good reasons are shown for believing that others resemble them, it is, I think, a fair inference, that the number of the inhabitants of the country is proportionately under-estimated.

For many years the population was given in official returns at less than 5,000,000, though Mr. Binning in 1850 estimated it at 8,000,000. Within the last four years it has been raised to 7,653,600 from an estimate made by an officer in the Shah's Government of admittedly the roughest possible character. No one perhaps is more competent to guess than the officer referred to, but a guess is a guess, and until all the unknown tracts have been traversed and described it is futile to make an estimate. A small and well-populated tract will make up for a large patch of desert. It is quite possible that another five millions, and not two and a half, should have been added to the old estimate. The Persian officials have no ideas on the subject, and supply no data on which reliance can be placed. As an instance of the trustworthiness of such estimates as have been made, I may mention that the average population is considered to be 7 per square mile now that the total population is estimated at 7,653,600, just as it was when the estimate was 4,400,000. Such instances might be multiplied. How can the population of the villages be set down at 3,780,000 when villages without number have never been visited by any official above the grade of a menial servant? Till 1881 it was as confidently asserted that the inhabitants of villages and country districts numbered 1,700,000. Is it probable that the country population should be so small as 3,780,000 in a country of such enormous extent—that extent, too, being probably under-estimated—where the necessaries of life are so cheap that large flat flaps of excellent bread form the table of the poor as well as their food, and where want is, the rare seasons of famine excepted, absolutely unknown? With these prefatory remarks as to impressions received before I left the road and confirmed on my journey, I proceed to note down the observations made on the way. I had a prismatic compass, a watch, and an aneroid barometer with me. Scanty materials for the roughest survey, yet I am informed on the best authority that much of the existing map of Persia rests on observations taken in this manner. A thermometer could not be obtained in the capital of the Shah, and I have in consequence no readings by which my barometrical observations can be corrected. I have given the estimate in feet corresponding to the degrees marked. The heights given are mere rough approximations. I shall enter the mileage in the margin so as to preserve an uninterrupted narrative, the observations taken being more clearly shown in the map annexed to these notes and in the itinerary, and I will now ask my reader to imagine himself with me at Kasveen after having been jolted in a tarantasse over the 98 miles that intervene between that place and Teheran. This is fortunately the only stage in Persia that can be done on wheels. A so-called carriage road has been lately made from Teheran to Kom also, but happily this was under water when I journeyed up. A carriage road is, I fear, in Persia only an excuse for taking of the post-horses and making the traveller drive, to his excessive discomfort and at an exorbitant cost.

Kasveen was well known in old crusading times as the nearest town to the mountain retreat of the Chief of the Assassins, the Old Man of the Mountains, in later times as the capital of Nadir Shah, and in modern times as the birth-place of Zareen Taj, the Crown of Gold, the ill-fated Hypatia of the Babees.

It has often been described, and I have nothing to say about it but that an official of the place who had just returned from Mashad told me that even in that stronghold of Islam a large proportion of the people were Babees at heart, and that I met a Russian there who had travelled all over Persia and Turkey (at whose expense was not clear) and who was now a Mussalman and a servant on some Rs. 20 a month to the Governor of Kasveen. The headman of one of the divisions of the town told me much about the Babees, and said, with reference to the recent diplomatic differences between Russia and England, that in Persia it was commonly believed that the English had set the Afghans up to fight the Russians. "In fact," he said, "پلتک کردند" (paltik kardand). This was obviously the English word Politics. Asked what it meant; he said he understood it was the equivalent of دروغ (dirogh), a lie.

No one here had travelled more than a *parasang** or two south or south-west, and I experienced much difficulty in hiring two horses, one for myself and another for my modest effects and a man I had picked up at Teheran, who professed to know something about the country. I had yet to learn that, during the month of Ramazan at any rate, wholesale bribery and offers of absurdly high remuneration will often fail to procure beasts of burden or induce a muleteer to move. With Ramazan impending, his heart begins to harden. Along a caravan track a muleteer is a servant; off it a capricious and unreasonable despot, who has to be coaxed and bribed to move a mile in any unknown direction. One man, after the contract was arranged, disappeared. After waiting a day I found he had no intention of coming. He told another, not myself, that he would not come. He had seen a look of violence in my eye at Kasveen. I might kill him in the unknown country. I was warned that the, people were fanatical, and recommended as a companion "a butcher who could knock down ten men." This did not seem to me the way to deal with fanatics, and I declined his services. Supplies would be most difficult to get: there was no fodder for horses; no Farangi had been across the hills of Ramand before; Dr. Pulak had gone with a caravan by Ab-i-garm; therefore I should.

However in the end we started, and, contrary to all custom, made a march instead of loading and mounting, riding through the city gate, and unloading and dismounting to see if anything had been forgotten.

Yet another word by way of preface.

If my observations as to the condition of the people have any value, it is to be attributed chiefly to the fact that I travelled absolutely without official aid and countenance and associated on terms of absolute equality with any one and everyone I met. I had a letter from the Minister of Foreign Affairs which I carefully concealed, and of the existence of which I kept my Persian attendant ignorant. Its use would have frozen up the fountain of confidence and have entitled me to camp anywhere without paying my way. Once let the possession of such a document be known and it is useless to attempt to pay your way. The money never gets to the owners of the things supplied you and the houses in which you sleep. They do not expect it in such a case. It is the custom of Iran for the officially protected to batten on the people, and a man who does not pay his way is at least as little liked among the grasping Persians as elsewhere. As a mere friendless traveller you learn more though you fare less well. Hence I determined to keep my letter for a serious emergency should any such occur, and, during my little exploring trip, to sleep where I could and eat what I could get, and trust to my knowledge of Persian and the Persians to see me through. Short though this little expedition was, it needed for its accomplishment all the experience I had gained in more extended travels over better known portions of the country.

figures of horsemen with spears and swords in hand, carved on upright, not recumbent, grave-stones. I was told there were 700 or 800 head of cattle in Farsian, and sheep innumerable.

From Farsian to Ajurband is a pleasant march through fields 11 miles. of barley and wheat, watered by underground irrigation channels. Just around the latter village white and yellow roses grow in such quantities as make the air heavy with their scent, and over this uncared-for garden and above the gate hangs from the village walls a little upper chamber wherein the traveller is allowed to rest. The village is small, say 50 houses, as many head of cattle and more sheep. The inhabitants are Turkis and the women, therefore, unveiled. The old peasant who did the honours told me that the Government demand had been raised and that the villagers were badly off. My informant had, however, seven daughters. I asked what they did. He said they slept and ate. The people looked well fed and well found as if they enjoyed a fair share of both these luxuries.

As usual a large crowd collected to see the Farangi eat his curds and cucumbers, his bread and cold fowl. I asked the old spokesman to join me, not having enough to go around, but he declined, as he was making up for a day's fast missed last year. This, from a man of at least 70, and with a June-July Ramazan impending. At parting I said to the crowd, "What do you think of the first Farangi who has visited your village," but the old man interposed and said, "How should they express opinions about God's works. Did not God make Farangi and Mussalman alike?" This answer made my apparently harmless question appear to myself frivolous and absurd.

I left the little village with its solemn grey-beard chief and 12½ miles. journeyed through barley and wheat past Hakimabad and Akhoora across an irrigation channel and through land either cultivated or cultivable to Shaintappa, a little village of 50 or 60 homes of Turki people. Here I found that 5 pence a day with food was the labourer's hire, that he got about 9 pence without it, and in the long days of July as much as 13 pence. I use English terms in preference to Persian, but they express in no way the purchasing power of the wage. I hesitate to express my opinion as to the difference in this respect between a franc and a kran. I shall be within the mark if I say that a family can be fed in Persia for what it costs to feed an individual in England. From information received here I calculated that 340 lb. of wheat and 430 lb. of barley could be purchased for about 7 shillings. The Mustehidd or high priest of Kasveen, who owns this village, gives the cultivators half the crop.

good glasses and medical advice to check incipient complaints would be an incalculable boon.

Next morning, leaving Saidabad and a tangle of adjacent villages, the bearings of which are given in the itinerary, we passed on to Juveen, leaving a watercourse on the left and on the right a vineyard, only to get on to others which surround the village. Not to deface this too monotonous narrative with statistics, Juveen is a walled village like the others already described, and with sheep and asses and horned cattle in much the same numbers. 19¼ miles.

From a hillock here the view across the plain northwards over the wheat, the villages, and the orchard trees, to the lofty snow capped Talághán, is very like that from the Punjab railway at Gujerat across to the Himalayas. Far away to the right the snowy peak of Demavend is only just visible at a distance of over 120 miles, and dwarfed as it now is to small proportions, it allows the Elburz range as a whole to stand out in its true grandeur. To the south the hills of Ramand, also capped with snow, shut in the fertile plain we traverse.

The villagers of Juveen complained that they were called on to pay more than the just dues of Government, because the Governor had offered more than the usual payment into the royal treasury. They struck me as being in very fair circumstances, and dotted around them were other villages which presented the same appearance.

Hardly are the crops of Juveen passed when Mahomedabad is reached, the only walled village, from the mud towers of which I have had a conversation with the ladies who dwell within. They were Turkis of course, Persian-speaking Turkis. My salaam was returned; my business asked. What did I make by this journey? Certainly I might put their pictures in my note-book if I liked. They might have added, if I could. My village was London was it, and where was that? The men would probably have known it well by name. They were all out at work in the fields. Hence this undisturbed flirtation from the walls. The head-man, however, soon appeared and said, Farangi, stay and breakfast here, we've water, shade, and all good cheer. It seemed a nice village, but I was as anxious to keep moving as he was to ask questions.

A hillock, a village—Idrabad—the tomb of a saint—how plentiful they were of old in Islam—these passed, and the river Kharood is reached. This stream irrigates places the underground channels do not reach, and helps in no small degree to maintain throughout the fertility of the plain of Kasveen. There might have been half a foot of water in the centre of a bed some

serpentinely corrugated iron, and to the west their surface is lumped into shapes like the rounded tops of domes and houses as seen when looking down on them from a minaret. Not one person in this village of perhaps 1,500 inhabitants could write. This is very unusual and was significant of our approach to the still wilder hills. Eastwards beyond this village extends for a long distance uncultivated waste. I had now crossed the plain of Kasveen from the Elburz to the Karaghan range. The reader will have seen that it is studded with villages covered with wheat, and dotted with vineyards and orchards.

Compare this two days' journey of 27 miles in all with that of two days anywhere between Bushire and Teheran. Allow 200 miles for the two days, and you will hardly pass so many villages and so much cultivation. All across the route I took, wheeled conveyances could be brought, supplies and water could be got, and carriage for large numbers by arrangement. There were very few asses and mules, and except at Dizan, a village I passed near but did not visit, no camels. Large numbers, however, were feeding up in the hills. Cows, bullocks, sheep and goats, and very inferior poultry abounded everywhere. Meat is only eaten by the well-to-do, and can only be bought by the pound or piece in large villages. Eggs, curds, cucumbers and flaps of unleavened bread can be got anywhere at a moment's notice. A little to the east of Ibrahimabad is a large village, Sagsabad, described in Walker's map as Sagziabad and in Kiepert's map as Sakizabad. There are many places about of names somewhat similar to this, and as the existence of Sagsabad seems to be hardly known at Kasveen, it is important that it should bear in the map a name which may, when used by travellers, be recognisable by the people. The name given is altogether misleading.

From Ibrahimabad the ascent to Ruak begins over slopes that are stoneless and sparsely grassy. We pass flocks of sheep and herds of cattle under the charge of shepherds camping in the thick, black, flat-topped felt tents used by nomad tribes in Persia.

Ruak is 7¼ miles from the foot of the hills, from which, how- 35 miles. ever, it is not visible. Two other villages on the hill-side to the west of it can be seen from long distances across the plain, and one or the other of these, I was assured on all hands, was Ruak, or as the Turkis call it, Rudak. A large and beautiful village it is, nestling in a fold in the hill-side, with wheat in terraces around and above and below it, and gardens such as I had not seen till then and did not see again till Hamadan was reached. Giant walnut trees, luxuriant vines, flourishing peach, cherry, and almond, and all kinds of fruit trees. Here my aneroid, which had stood at 4,500 at Ibrahimabad, had risen to 6,000.

The local estimate of the distance hence to Kasveen was 9 farsakhs. My calculation was 35 miles, which is as nearly as may be the same thing. The ascent was very gradual and could easily be made practicable for wheels.

Before, during, and after dinner the usual process of cross-examining went on. I found it a very paying procedure to let the people examine me. One learnt so what their minds were running on.

A villager who had lived in Teheran, and another who had lived in the capital and Bushire, naturally became the spokesmen. With the former, " Is it true that all America (the young world) belongs to the Russians (Ooroos) ? " " Very far from true ; much of it belongs to the English ; none to the Russians." "Ah, I heard differently in Teheran." " Who is Shah of Hindustan ? " " Our Queen." Sensation. " What about the brother of the King of India who lives at Baghdad ?" " He is not the king's brother ; there is no such king. He is the relation of a king who formerly ruled over a very small portion of India." This referred to the Nawab Ikbal-ud-doulah, who sat for ten days on the throne of Oudh. " Was India big ? " " Very, very big." " How big ?" " Twice as long and twice as broad as Persia, with twenty-five times its population at the least, and with a dozen cities greater than Teheran or Tabriz, and half a hundred larger than Ispahan." I had these facts ready, as such questions had occurred often during my travels. I spoke the truth so far as I could find it out, but what appeared so magnificent an exaggeration, completely upset my questioner, who said no more.

The Bushire man then took me in hand and asked me much about the prices of the necessaries of life in England, marvelling with the rest of the audience at the wealth of a people who could pay them. I did not tell him it is no uncommon thing for the poor there to suffer actual want in the midst of this wealth. He seemed worth examining in return, so I asked him—seeing I was a mere traveller and no official, as they could see by the absence of baggage and servants—to tell me the truth, did he and most of his countrymen like the Inglees. I begged him as a favour to give me his candid opinion. He did not like them, nor did his countrymen. Why ? In answer. " Do you like the Persians ? your candid opinion ?" " Well "—pause—" not the Persians of the towns, because "—" Enough ; I see you don't like them. My reasons for not liking the English are the same as yours for not liking us."

This man had been a soldier and served long years at most of the big military centres. He was not a mere gossip. In his opinion a cultivator in his village could live and bring up a family on 10 tomans, say £3-7-0, a year.

The audience departs, the traveller lies down; and now the nightly visitors begin. Cats come trying to lift the brass plate off the milk; dogs come sniffing at the Farangi; fleas and vermin, the curse *par excellence* of the country, commence their attacks. Turning around on my pillow after a broken sleep, my cheeks grate on what turns out to be the skeleton of the fowl that had furnished my dinner, which some dog or cat had stolen, picked, and honestly returned.

Two miles hence next morning along a path skirting a channel fringed with grass, clover and forget-me-not, we rode to Alakaseer or Rustamabad, so called, not after Rustam the son of Zal, but after Rustam of the one hand—whoever he may have been. Most villages in this hill country have a Turki and a Persian name. Past Alakaseer runs down to the plains by Sagsabad a fairly considerable stream. Around the village for miles are vineyards and orchards hardly less beautiful than those of Ruak. Entering the little street, we meet a small boy who naïvely calls out "Did you see my father in Teheran?" None of these villages boast any manufacturers. The blacksmith and carpenter and shoemaker—the indispensable artisans—are alone to be found. The men are clad in tunics of piece-goods dyed blue and felt caps; the women in piece-goods cloths, the skirt of the hardy Turki woman not differing in any essential from that of her European sister peasant. The hideous trouser cloth and veil disguise of females on the plains is not met with henceforward till we reach Hamadan, for we are now in the country of Turkis and nomad tribes. *37 miles.*

The pulses just cut are here placed to dry on the house-tops, and they serve as an excellent bed on which to spread a sleeping rug.

I make Alakaseer to be 6,000 feet above the sea. Neither hence nor from Ruak can you see aught but the little mountain valley, in the light green folds of which, as they descend to the river, lie vineyards of a brighter and orchards of a darker green.

Half a mile's ride, however, up a gentle ascent, alongside walled gardens, brings the traveller to Yeryan, a hamlet belonging to Alakaseer, whence a strikingly beautiful view is obtained. Below, the river, fringed with willows and plane trees, winds down between vineyards and orchards to Ruak. On the east, close at hand, is a wavy hill-side not unlike the treeless downs of the *37¼ miles.*

Nílgiris, above which, shutting out the further view in that direction, rises the crest of the mountain, broken into little peaks, while fifty miles away, across the invisible plain we have traversed in the last two days, the pure white snow on the tops of the Elburz sparkles in the morning sun. Along the banks of the brook that skirts the pathway is a fringe of turf pranked with clover white and red, dandelion, and a little yellow flower resembling the immortelle. The shade of walnut, plane and mulberry trees wards off, for alas! too short a distance, the rays of a fierce sun, and the strong-scented *sinjit* tree perfumes the air in all directions. In a spot like this one can well understand how the walled garden became the earthly prototype of a paradise where shade and rest are lasting and not a brief incident in a long and stony road.

40¼ miles. Three miles further on a mountain stream from the west joins the Ruak river near Yalghoon in a barren mountain pass.

43 miles. We turn here to the west up a long sloping valley, crowning which in the far distance is Chenarah or Plane Tree Village, a village, however, without a single plane, a pastoral hamlet, with wheat and fruit enough for its own consumption.

47 miles. In the four further miles we ride to reach Chenarah, the ruins of a village and the encampment of a nomad tribe are passed. Here I had to settle a quarrel between my muleteer and one of the Eels. The dogs rushed out of the black tents on our approach. I was mounted and held my ground; the muleteer, who was on foot, drew his sword and made to use it against his assailants, who were fierce enough to justify some such move. Thereon, however, the owner clubbed his long musket and made for the muleteer, who gave way a little. A fight was the thing of all others to be avoided, and I rushed at my man, who, being a Persian, had no real stomach for a fight, and only maintained a threatening attitude with his sword drawn from fear of the dogs. Had he actually slashed them, I don't think I could have saved him a severe mauling from the infuriated Eel. This muleteer— I call him so though he supplied me with two horses only—was always trying by his own boastful and overbearing demeanour to make up for the absence of any pretension on my part and for the scantiness of my belongings, of which he was, I believe, honestly ashamed. Pomp and circumstance is the very breath of a Persian's nostrils.

From Ibrahimabad on the plains, up to this point, where the aneroid marks 7,300 feet, the ascent is gradual, and a road fit for wheels might easily be constructed. From Alakaseer onwards, however, come long stretches of barren hills, where the little villages could afford supplies for a small party only.

Camels were feeding in large numbers on the hill-sides, which presented now a blue, now a red, and now a purple appearance, which must be due to peculiarities in the soil, the vegetation here being sparse and uniform. Doubtless these were indications of metallic wealth below.

From Chenarah we go up and down over barren, undulating hills, now and again catching a peep of the Elburz, for four miles, when we get to the Koh-i-Ramand, a hill famed for its herbs 51 miles. throughout Western and Central Asia and away to distant Hindustan. So at least I am informed, and the peculiar character of the vegetation would strike the most careless and unskilled observer. The ascent lies along the bank of a big brawling stream of the clearest water, fed by springs at intervals on its way. On either side stretches a fringe of turf of unusual breadth, and beyond this the hill-sides are grassy—the first hill-sides I had seen that deserved the name. Scented wild thyme grows profusely here, and the iris, butter-cup, dandelion, blue-bell, forget-me-not, mallow, and other common English flowers, grow side by side with others whose names I know not, of a most un-English character.

Nothing is so extraordinary in travelling in these parts as the sudden changes of temperature and scenery. To-day we started from the lovely villages of Ruak and Alakaseer. No sooner were these left behind than miles of stony road led through barren hills, which reflected the sun's rays with painful intensity, to Chenarah, whence, after crossing a breezy height, more stony barren road led to this protected hill-side, clothed with grass, covered with springs and adorned by flowers. At the top of Koh-i-Ramand the aneroid marked 8,000, and thence a short but abrupt descent 52¼ miles. brought us to Sumeinak, a tiny Eel village, possessed however of a garden 'rude in uncultivated loveliness.'

Here dwelt an aged Khan, who, with all the men in the village, came and sat under the tree where I ate my breakfast. While I bathed under a small cascade of icy water hard by, he had had a soup made for me of onions, vinegar, and some other ingredient I could not recognise. He begged me to stay there while a kid was converted into roast. I declined and asked after his health. This is done at intervals in Persian society as well as at meeting. It is the equivalent to the English weather. He answered me seriously enough however, "I am old, I am ill, my eyes are dim, I have many enemies." He then told me that he had been the Khan of the chief Eel or tribe of those parts, and had been deposed in favour of his younger brother, who had more money for bribing at Court than himself. I afterwards learnt, however, that he had been a disobedient son, this aged Khan, disinherited by his father and not deposed by the Shah. He spoke as if his misfortunes had been of yesterday, and from his sad appearance I can well believe that they had been ever present in his mind.' He asked for my boots, but as I had only one pair I could not give them up. This was not the request of poverty, though he was poor enough. The porpoise hide and thick soles attracted him. Suddenly an idea struck me. I had in my saddle-bags one little tin of sweet biscuits given me at Teheran. It was opened with a sharp stone, and biscuit by biscuit, for greater politeness, handed by me to the Khan and his sons. They were much liked. Colonel Burnaby recommended Cockle's pills for Turkey: I humbly suggest sweet biscuits for Persia.

When I was packing my saddle-bags to move on, the Khan made a request. He wanted the biscuit tin. Then we walked up the garden, and reached the low monolith door of egress, he holding one of my hands in one of his, and the empty biscuit tin in the other. At the door I stood aside to let the old man pass through first. His sons and the villagers stood in rows on either side. It was an impromptu patriarchal function. As he stooped with difficulty to pass through the low doorway, it was impossible not to admire the simple dignity which was not impaired by association with an empty biscuit tin. I protest, in spite of the humour of it, I entirely shared in the obvious respect and compassion of his few poor retainers.

To this mountain of Ramand come mysterious dervishes or fakirs from Hindustan. They take out bread and the coarse hill cheese, and stay out in the mountains for perhaps a week, perhaps a fortnight, perhaps a longer time, till they find the herbs they want, when they are off again. The Khan assured me they have been known to compass wonderful cures. That men answering the description given do come for herbs, of the properties or supposed properties of which others are ignorant, I see no reason to doubt. Indeed I think these mysterious persons cannot be satisfactorily disposed of, as they often are, by the lightly made assertion, that they are gross impostors and no more.

Hence it is nearly a parasang through stony barren hills to Razzak, a poor village, possessed of a little unirrigated wheat. Beyond this an event happened.. I met another traveller—a Seyyad collecting his tithes. He was entitled, he said, just at this time, to a certain quantity of milk or its value and a certain number of fleeces or their value. He lived at Kulanjeen, where I was to sleep, but would offer me no advice or help as to a night's

56 miles.

lodging. Of course there are no Babees among the ignorant old-world people of the hills. Still it seemed odd that this descendant of the Prophet should have known nothing of a movement of such vital moment to Islam.

After passing three small Eel villages, and a hill stream flowing west, the garden of Kulanjeen, and then the village itself, is reached, eleven miles from Razzak. The population of this place cannot be short of 3,000, and its flocks are proportionately numerous. No camels belong to the people, but numbers which I have no means of ascertaining, the property of the nomad tribes, were grazing about the surrounding hills. 67 miles.

Below the village runs the river of Karaghan, the chief stream that drains these hills, and on its banks, a mile to the west, is Misrabad, perhaps half the size of Kulanjeen. Thereabouts grow good crops of barley, wheat, peas and melons. The species of poplar, locally known as Sufeydar-i-Tabreezi, has been largely planted, and its wood is cut into planks and used for house-building.

I make the height here 7,300 feet. There were many large Persian houses in the village, but the only lodging I could get was in a foul room adjoining a stable, where I spent a sleepless night.

It will not be forgotten that I was travelling as a wandering European on my own resources. A sight of the concealed letter would have obtained for me the best lodging the place afforded, but for reasons I have given I had determined to see exactly what I could get on my own merits and what the attitude of the people to an unprotected European really was.

From Kulanjeen the path goes down through a fold in the hills to a valley through which the Kharjistan river flows to join the Karaghan river at Misrabad. A curiously red hill, probably metalliferous, faces you as you descend to the river level. Four and a half miles beyond Meylakh is reached, a small village, near which are some lofty rocks, whence grows a walnut tree pointed out by the people as a great curiosity. The ravens who live in the rocks had carried the seed up there. On the west side of the stream is a giant rose tree and hard by a small but neat little building with a dome. This was the tomb of the last owner of the village. He had been a man of wealth and fashion, a dweller in the capital, but falling sick had left wife and children to come to his hill estate and recover in the cool mountain air. He got nothing better, however, but rather worse, and died suddenly ere he could arrange for the interment of his body at Mashad, Kerbela, or Kom. His heirs, glad of an omission that spared their pocket, buried him 68¼ miles.

here beside the stream in the lonely mountain ravine where, instead of the company of myriads of believers whose bones crumble around the shrines of the holy Imams, he gets, what in life he would have despised, the passing sympathy of a solitary Farangi. Not 100 miles off at Kom sleeps an Imam's sister, 500 miles on either side of him the blessed Imams themselves. Truly his destiny was unpropitious. Let us hope that

" After life's fitful fever he sleeps well."

75 miles. Ooroo was next reached, a picturesque village where we could learn nothing about our further route. On the way here an old peasant on a laden mule, to whom I gave the inside of the narrow path hanging over the river, gave me so little law that he shoved me on to the edge of the path, over which nothing but the extraordinary sure-footedness of my horse saved my going. The path is difficult and dangerous. Hence we ascended to 8,800 feet to a
78 miles. point from which a vast expanse of furrowed and broken hill country was visible, and then made for Haráeen-i-suflah, a small hamlet of some 60 houses, at an elevation of 8,000 feet, with no gardens, but with some wheat cultivation. The inhabitants say they have enough to go on with and no more. All around here the hills are stony and barren. Rain-fed wheat, however, is to be found near all the hamlets, and three such can be seen from Haráeen.

And now we have to march over the highest point attained on this little expedition, 9,700 feet. To reach this we pursue a path just negociable with care by horses and crowning a precipitous descent. Then comes a hard climb to the top, where snow drift still robs the hardy camels of part of the scanty herbage they seek. The view hence of the country travelled over in the day was dreary beyond description. Far away north appeared the snowy Elburz, nearer south the snowy Elwand, to the foot of which I am bound. East and west range upon range of treeless and unfriendly looking hills. The villages of Upper and Lower Haraina, straight lines of mud huts, set in an arid background of hillside, only accentuated the desolate character of the view. Who would believe that the smiling gardens of Ruak were so near?

88 miles. Over the crest of the hill, however, matters suddenly improve, and 1,000 feet lower down is the Turki hamlet of Shah-bulaghee, said by the villagers to be 20 miles from Kulanjeen. My calculations it will be seen by the figures in the margin agree as nearly as possible with this estimate.

Before getting to the village we fell in with an encampment of Turki Eelyats, and as no supplies could be raised at Haraina, where I had breakfasted, I got a good meal of cheese, bread, and milk in the black tents. Accustomed as I had now become to the Persian system of not only paying, but paying exorbitantly, for hospitality, I proferred a franc piece, but my host said with dignity in Turki, "We do not sell the produce of our flocks; you are welcome to be our guest." I had not acquired enough Turki to answer, so asked my man to say "that it was thus in our country, and that I was very sensible of my entertainer's feeling in the matter." This was thus translated: "The Farangi Saheb says it is just like this in the country of London. No one there pays for anything."

After this I commended my host to God's protection, the local good-bye, and went my way to the village.

My companion's speech as an interpreter suggests to me a few words on Persian geography. I speak, of course, of the uninformed or only slightly illuminated.

The great country of Farangistan, where men travel hundreds of parasangs a day on the iron road, is divided into two portions, one Francistan and one Inglistan, which is either the capital of London or of which London is the capital. Near this is the far larger country of the Ooroos, while in some ill-defined direction is the young world in which generally very little interest is taken.

As to the politics of these countries knowledge and speculation is confined to the Inglees and the Ooroos. The existence of two parties among the former, named Vig and Toaree, is better known than might be expected; still such knowledge is confined to the local politician or the rural khan. These parties are understood to be constantly at war with one another, while the Ooroos is more rationally governed by a Shah, who does not allow civil war. The Inglees lately suffered a defeat in Egypt at the hands of the Mahdi, but have been successful in setting up the Afghans to fight the Russians near Herat, which it is their intention to seize. It is by no means thought that the English are always outwitted. Rather is the *perfide Albion* theory held. The probability of war with Russia was widely known. A Persian, Arab or Turki will ever seize the opportunity afforded by meeting a foreigner to learn all he can about this subject and to show that in such matters he is chiefly interested. It must be remembered that the views on politics and geography I have just repeated are those of persons I met on this little tour in remote plains and in Turki hill villages, not of the people of Shiraz, Ispahan, and Teheran. I need not say more. At the very village I have got to, the spokesman said that to see a Farangi was like a dream. I use the word Farangi, which in Persia implies nothing of contempt as Feringhee does in India. The word Kafir, on the other hand, should never be applied by an Englishmen to himself. I once did apply the expression in pleasantry to the English and was rebuked in these words: "The followers of His Highness Jesus, on whom be peace, are not Kafirs. Why fix on yourselves an epithet your enemies would not apply to you."

One of the best authorities in India, however, lately pointed out in vain the impolicy of the acceptance of such a name. He was answered by the light of philology, but not, I think, by that of experience.

To return to Shahbulagee. Its dozen houses were almost in ruins. The cause? A party of the Soldooz tribe, who live near Sava in the winter and roam all over Irak in the summer, had been raiding lately and had taken 100 of their sheep. A fight ensuing, the village had suffered. Would they not complain to the Governor? No. Did they do nothing? Yes, they had got back their sheep! How? "By asking for them. We said we are miserably poor. They said, 'you are poor devils,' and they killed two lambs for dinner and gave us back the rest."

If this appears improbable, let it not be forgotten that after all robbers only exist on sufferance. I have known occurrences not altogether unlike this in the case of gang robberies in the Marava country of Southern India. There is a code among a tribe of professional robbers that is not observed by casuals and amateurs.

90 miles.   Two miles further on, at Ainabad, I spent the night at the house of the village khan, who explained, *apropos* of the affair just mentioned that the raiding tribe was under the jurisdiction of the Naib-us-Sultanat, the village under the Zil-es-Sultan whose authority extends just so far. Hence these troubles. Had the Zil-es-Sultan, the Shah's eldest son, the undivided jurisdiction, such robbery and violence would not be tolerated.

From all I have seen and heard of this prince, I think this assumption quite justifiable. He is in fact a man of strong individuality, who is feared throughout the length and breadth of the wide provinces he governs. He has almost stamped out robbery and murder on the plains and established an understanding with the nomad tribes, who can only be ruled by more or less of compromise and agreement. He has vastly improved the army in equipment and drill and is passionately devoted to soldiering. In the English press I have seen it stated that he openly expresses his intention of trying to supplant his younger brother, the heir apparent, who is, unlike himself, on both sides of royal blood. That he expresses such an intention is certainly untrue. He is far too discreet. Moreover, he pays all respect to the heir apparent, and lately, when the latter rode past his new palace at Teheran, he waited for him and placed its title-deeds in his hands. All he had was the heir apparent's. The latter prince, however, had the deeds transferred to the giver's son with similar expressions of respect and good will. As to the Zil-es-Sultan's intentions, they are best known to himself. Speculation of course is busy in respect of a prince who is Governor of half Persia, the Shah's eldest son, and the ablest and most powerful man in the country.

Some idea of this personage may be obtained from the following brief account of an interview with him. Scene, the palace garden at Ispahan. *Dramatis personæ*, the prince, commander of army corps, officers, courtiers, secretaries, a guard of soldiers, myself—a large company. Was I in the army? No. A pity. Aside to the others but in the same tone, "A good youth." Hereon I tried to look my best. I had apologised, on being presented, for the costume of the traveller. What was I travelling for? "To learn Persian and see the country." Aside "Just like these Englishmen." To me "Why do they want to know so much? Here no one knows anything. It is better so. I know nothing, but I can govern provinces." An assent *more Persico* from me. "What about the Russian crisis?" "I have no news of late, but I believe there will be no war." "It is certain there will be none." "I had not heard that." "And if there were war, who would conquer?" "Please God, the English." "I hope they may."

The prince was not serious in saying that he and his people knew nothing. In the towns the average of elementary education is high, and higher education is by no means neglected. A tutor is a matter of course in a family which can afford one.

If then the nomad tribes have preserved intact, as is alleged, the customs they observed in the time and before the time of Alexander the Great, yet has one of their most cherished customs, viz., that of plundering their neighbours, been much proscribed in these present times. Were the Zil-es-Sultan supreme, he would soon stamp it out of the whole country.

Ainabad is a fertile little village at the foot of the hills we have come over. The khan tells me that the Soldooz above mentioned come down occasionally and pasture their flocks and herds on his lands, but apparently they are moderate in their behaviour. At any rate the khan spoke with little resentment.

In Persia, even more than in India, I think servants are the friends and companions of their masters, who are led by them to an extent hardly intelligible to an European. I have explained that I fared in the same way as my two companions all along the route, and I should have said the distance between us was reduced to a minimum. The khan, however, thought otherwise. He and his brother and I were sitting on a carpet taking tea before dinner. Two of the women of the family were still carpet-making in an adjoining big hall, two more were standing in the door way listening to our talk. "A petition" said the khan. "It is granted," said I. "Your muleteer and man have travelled far to-day." "Yes," said I, not understanding him, "My man rode on the pack-horse, but we could not get a donkey for the muleteer. We saw many, but a week's wage for a day's work failed to induce the fasting owners to come over the hills." (It was Ramazan). "Yes, but your men will want to sit down." "With all my heart. I don't want them. I think they are standing here to listen for their own amusement." "Yes, but they can't listen standing. Mayn't they sit on *our* carpet?" "Certainly." So they sat on the small square carpet and the muleteer at once began his usual unfavourable comparison between me and my saddle bags and Hakeem (Dr.) Pulak with his tents, his baggage mules, and his servants. If I could not afford to travel like that, why didn't I go to Hamadan by the road on which travelling in this way was less expensive and less dangerous. He would have given me half a dozen horses to have gone by the road and so on. I was sick of him, but the khan considered he had as much right to the attention of the company as himself or myself. I note this as it illustrates the treatment of servants and the license of speech usual throughout a country where liberty is said to be unknown and the poor to be universally oppressed.

Another speech of the khan's will, I think, bear repetition. I asked "How many children have you?" Looking to his brother he answered, "We have five."

Looking back on the hills already traversed, it will be remembered that they are dotted with villages of hardy and well-fed Turkis and encampments of Eels, and would grow far more rain-irrigated wheat than they do if it was sown. Some of these villages have fair, some beautiful gardens, producing enough fruit for their own consumption and for despatch to the villages below, the grapes in particular being transported in large quantities to Resht on the Caspian. Pasture, for the most part poor in quality, exists in quantity sufficient for an infinite number of camels and for large flocks of sheep and herds of cattle. Along the frequent streams irrigated wheat is found.

Are all these remote villages—many of them quite little towns—taken into account in the 3,780,000 estimate of the population of villages and towns? I think not.

The hills seemed to contain but little animal life. Of birds, I saw vultures, ravens, the red-headed wood-pecker, and the ubiquitous sparrow. Crabs and tortoises were common; water-snakes less so. Insects abounded of all sorts, including the tarantula. Of land snakes I saw none.

Across the plain of Kasveen, say 40 miles, a road could easily be constructed, and across the 50 miles of hill it could perhaps with a little engineering be continued.

Now comes another plain similar in character, but smaller in extent, than that of Kasveen. In this locality much carpet-making goes on. A carpet, large enough for a small English breakfast-room, will run from £20 to £30, more of course being asked. It must, too, be made to order, as the Persians like their carpets in strips as broad as a wide staircase, but no broader.

Through irrigated wheat mingled with poppies, a path leads 91¼ miles. from Ainabad to Shavand, a little village with a little vineyard and a rural khan, whose house seemed all too great for his estate, boasting a small tower, a large Persian window with little panes of glass set in trellis wood-work and a pretty lawn whereon grew apple and cherry trees and a scentless mignonette.

There was no shop, no bazaar, in this village of 200 houses. Nothing was exported; the grapes and the wheat fed the labourers who grew them and kept the khan going; no more. The land seemed well suited to opium, but the villagers said, "they had not yet learnt that cultivation."

Barley and pulses grew all along to Razeen, 4½ miles further on 96 miles. where I breakfasted at the earnest solicitation of the village khan, who said there was no such garden and no such upper chamber as his nearer than Hamadan. He took me all over his house and left me talking to his wife, his brother's wife, and their daughters while he busied himself with preparing for my entertainment, which was to be on rather a grand scale. First I had to go through the usual ordeal of medical advice, protesting abysmal ignorance of the subject the while. A queer case I had to treat here. The khan's mother suffered from bad eyes. I had not a drug but quinine with me, but she implored me to recommend something. Perforce I went into the case. How long had her eyes been bad? For three years. How old was she? 60. Being a khan's mother she had no out-door work to do? No. If it was not sun I could not guess the cause or advise anything. But the cause is well known said she. Indeed, what? "I wept so when my youngest son was taken from home to be a soldier." I hoped her son might be restored to her, and felt the cold water cure, my stock prescription for bad eyes, to be out of place with this poor old lady. The other women of the family had a big carpet on the primitive loom. My host had one wife. Very rarely has any one hereabouts two or more. Indeed through Persia one wife is the rule.

Near here is Darjazeen, which is marked in Walker's map, but called Durgazeen. An Imamzadah with a high tower marks its site. I am told here that it was once a large place, but Nadir Shah had destroyed it because its inhabitants were obstinate Shias.

The khan's uncle collected a large crowd of his friends who as a favour allowed me by agreement ten minutes of my own company for bathing in the irrigation channel which ran through the garden. Before I could get on much clothing however, their curiosity brought them all around me and the khan's uncle noticing that my legs, feet, arms, hands, and face were alike covered with bites and stings, I sorrowfully said that there was no country in the world where a traveller was so tormented in this respect as Persia. "How else," said he, "'tis the country of Nasr-ud-din Shah." Was this meant in compliment to the king. "How else (دگر), could aught be said in any other spirit of the centre of the world's adoration." No, no, but still I did not understand. With one look around he fixed the audience, and while I struggled behind my coat into my riding breeches with my back to a tree he said, "These insects are as good as a daily bleeding. No man can be bled daily. Praise be to God who has devised this substitute."

Apropos of bleeding, it is very odd to see four or five men squatting contentedly by a barber's shop, each holding one forearm, from which the blood drips, over the gutter. I don't think the operation is so much resorted to in the villages. At any rate it only came under my notice in big towns. Hence, perhaps, the extraordinary speech quoted above. My friend was a man of much acuteness. He discovered in me a doctor, curing people for love of doing good (certainly I got no payment). He informed me that there was not a Babee left in Persia; that the Mahdi had driven the English out of Egypt; that he knew at once that I was not what I pretended to be, because if I came from Hindustan how could I speak Persian. Lest this frank confession of disbelief on the part of a yeoman appear offensive, let me quote a little episode from the best society in Persia. I was talking to a young prince of 16, already a governor, and said casually that I should see his father. Bye and bye I asked if he liked sport. Yes, said he in French, "mais je préfère mes études." I repeated this, as was obviously expected of me, to his father, who was delighted, and before all his approving courtiers said with a loud laugh " دروغ گفته است (Dirogh gufta ast) he lied."

The villages here are not, like those on the plain of Kasveen, surrounded by walls with watch-towers and entered by a single gate with a narrow roadway underneath, which turns at least once at right angles. The Kurds, they say, never raid in this direction. It will be remembered the Soldooz raided within a few days of my arrival at Shahbulághee not ten miles off. Formerly the Kurds had plundered freely in the plain of Kasveen. They do not do so now, but the statement suggested a romantic explanation of the bones so often noticed in the mud walls of the villages on the Kasveen side. There is no essential difference in the character of the houses in either plain. They are of the usual flat-roofed, mud-built character. A few cooking utensils, brass trays, often neatly engraved, skins for the manufacture and storing of curds, a rough carpet and a loom, make up the furniture of the ordinary peasant's house. The yeoman, khan or village headman's house is much bigger, has a yard and an upper story and better carpets, but its furniture is the same.

There is nothing to shoot on hill or plain but pigeons and partridges, nothing that can be easily got at. There are deer I am told, but I saw none.

From Rajeen past two hills much alike and hence called " The Brothers," past Aman and Darjazeen; a journey of half a parasang brings us to Karwah, where, under a spreading tree, the grey beards of the village were sitting at 3 p.m. listening to the Koran read by one of their number. I had not seen anywhere else a scene so suggestive of the village elders meeting at the "stone of discussion" in a Telugu village for gossip or deliberation. Under the tree a platform had been constructed, such as is often seen around the banyan and peepul in India. There was nothing odd about this, but I had not seen anything of the sort between the Persian Gulf and the Caspian, and it recalled at the moment far distant and far different scenes, as did the buttercups and forget-me-nots on the hill of Ramand. 98 miles.

A little cotton here varies the wheat, the pulses and the vines.

Another farsakh to another village Sayan, whence Harian is reached. Wheat extends along almost the whole distance, and villages, some only of which are named in the itinerary, are dotted all over the plain. Before reaching Farmineen, a village 102 miles. 105 miles. 117 miles.

of 2,000 to 3,000 inhabitants, my resting-place for the night, 12 more miles had to be traversed, the latter portion of the journey being over a grassy plain, covered with flocks and herds of sheep and cattle and camels.

These were slow long miles, and it was ½ past 9 on a dark night when our party of three souls got to the village. In Ramazan, and in the country at most times, I think, the evening meal is eaten as soon as the redness of the setting sun fades out of the sky. At any rate every house was closed and we seemed no nearer shelter than when out in the plain. The muleteer frightened away by his roughness the only inhabitant we captured. After some loss of time and three ineffectual attempts to get a hearing through barred doors, the existence of a Haji was mentioned and to him we went. He did not refuse to dispense some Persian hospitality, remuneration being agreed on before the door was opened. The old man was, with his son, plucking rose leaves, a huge heap of which lay by his side. At ½ past 11 some dinner was produced. The old man would say nothing, but "It's not bad" (بد نیست) and "There's no harm" (چه عیب دارد). What sort of a place was Mecca. "Not bad." A very good thing to have been there at any rate. "No harm." You must have a very high reputation in consequence. "Not bad." Not another word would he utter. In the morning I said: "I propose to give you this money as a small return for your hospitality." "There will be no harm." No, said I, "It's not bad." We left him. Much of the Shah's money, however, is bad, the new milled coinage being of far inferior silver to the old picturesque and irregular kran. Gold has disappeared from circulation, partly to be hoarded up and partly to pay for the great excess of imports over exports.

120 miles. Passing the Gulyuga Dágh, a curious hill with a flat-topped table-shaped brother beside it, Janabad comes in sight, a small village with one single manufacturer, who makes blue stoneware saltcellars and had a blue plate let into the wall over his door in the manner in which people delight in decorating their rooms in more civilised countries.

Near Janabad the track from Teheran to Hamadan passes, and it was open to me go around the hills by the road or straight over them. Robbers were said to hang about the hill road, which is very lonely. Not much believing in the robbers I decided on the latter route. "*Cantabit vacuus,*" said I. "But the horses are mine," said the muleteer.

124 miles. He had more reason to be apprehensive than I thought. A farsakh further on, at Nudah, at the foot of the range of low hills yet to be crossed, we come on six mounted ghulams or troopers

of the Shah, festooned with belts and cross-belts, well supplied with cartridges, and carrying each his gun, sword and pistol.

Six mounted robbers had, it seemed, a few days before attacked a muleteer who was taking the short cut across the hills with his mules, nine souls, some money and some merchandise. The muleteer, who had resisted and shot at his assailants, had been badly wounded, his mules, goods and money carried off.

The ghulams had come to catch these bold offenders, supposed to be Kurds of Kermanshah. One ghulam was coming on to Eedali, a ruin up the hill side, so we jogged along together, trying to converse, he in Turki, I in Persian.

At Eedali three travellers were sitting on a ruined hut. To them the ghulam said, "Why sit ye here sons of dogs. If ye are killed or robbed am I not responsible to Nasr-ud-din Shah ? Haste on to Janabad."

More stony hillside and we get to Goorjoos, a hideous village 134 miles. without a tree and only distinguishable at a distance as lumps of mud in the middle of some irrigated and unirrigated wheat. This place is nearly 7,000 feet above the sea level and looks the abomination of desolation. The villagers, however, about 60, all told, said the soil was very good and that they would not care to change lots with their neighbours in the fertile plain below. They said too, but their numbers are vague, that they had 30 cows and 1,000 sheep among them. I gathered the market value of a ploughing bullock to be £2-5-0, of a milch cow £1-10-0, of a two-storied mud house £18. The plentiful supply of milk obtained from goats explains the low price of the milch cow.

In a house here lay the victim of the Kurdish robbers with a bullet in one of his legs, which, so far as I could understand, the Turki medicine man had no intention of extracting. The wound was plastered over with some nauseous mixture of oil and herbs. I asked if anything was wanted and was told in a word "money." I gave some and reluctantly left the poor man. There was no doctor nearer than Teheran and no means of sending to Teheran a man who could not sit on a beast to ride there. Wheels there are none.

Eight miles more, along the barren mountain valley, past Aujabad and Kirmis Kharaba and over a height at one point between these villages of 7,500, and then comes a glimpse of the happy little valley of Hamadan, overshadowed by lofty Orontes with his snow-clad summit, covered with clumps of trees, each of which contains a fertile village, and watered by plenteous streams from the surrounding hills.

144 miles.   Half a farsakh more and the plain is entered, and a new Persia bursts on the astonished traveller far fairer than Shiraz, the seat of learning, or Ispahan, the crown of Islam, or Teheran, the foot-stool of royalty. Here in abundance and without alloy are all the beauties which few and far between cheer the weary traveller as he posts or caravans through the endless plains and over the everlasting mountains of this vast country.

I wish I could do justice to the view of the approach to Hamadan on a June afternoon. How different to the neighbourhood of the capital, desert to the very walls, nay in part within them. Here, no sooner are the hills left behind than down through vines you come to Surkhabad, where streams of crystal water ripple over pebbly beds, past vineyards whose low walls do not hide the light green foliage that rejoices in a milder sun. Huge storks strut solemnly about the lanes knowing that no impious hand will cast a stone at the bird who yearly earns the Haji's honoured name. Soft white clover lines the brookside, poppies as elsewhere mingle gaily with the wheat, thyme scents the air, and in shady summer-houses slumber the comfortable dwellers in this eastern Auburn. The river, wonder of wonders in this land of ruins, is spanned by a neat and useable bridge that does not end on either side in shallow water, and on the green banks feed fat flocks and sprawl lazy shepherds. The orchards are loaded with fruit, as yet unripe. The labourers are at work in the fields, their masters asleep, their women invisible, the shady lanes deserted but for the storks and the children, who love here, as all over the world, to dam up the water of the little rills and project it in tiny floods over the path.

Between this and Hamadan are three villages no less beautiful —Mehrabad, Amirabad, and Shuvareen—renowned for luscious grapes and situated on a slightly higher level whence the whole plain can be seen. No doubt long travel over desert wastes in a burning sun enhanced the concentrated beauty of this scene, but in no case could it fail to strike the observer. Three successive ranges of mountains break off from Elwand, the old Orontes, whose snowy top sparkles under the brightest of suns in the purest and most cloudless of blue skies. On every side hills appear to shut in this favoured spot from the outside world, and at the foot of the highest lies Hamadan, the ancient Ecbatana, hidden in trees. The afternoon sun grows milder, and a breeze, cooled in its passage over the mountains, ripples over the sea of tall waving wheat, which is broken only by clumps of fruit trees, vineyards and villages such as I have attempted to describe. The climate is no less superior to any other I have experienced in Persia. Ferdousi's description of the city of Kung might well apply to it :—

كرمش لـ كرمى بود وسردش لـ سرد

" Warmth without heat and coolness without chill."

Small wonder was it that the kings of the Assyrians coveted this retreat from the scorching summer plains of Babylon, and that the kings of the Medes made it their hot-weather capital. The very stones on the road were not as other stones, but largely mixed with a marble-like white quartz, which the excited imagination of a tired traveller, with the tomb of Esther and Mordecai before him, might almost take for the fragments of the palaces of aforetime, of Shusan the palace, the far off pleasure-house of Ahasuerus the king.

The setting sun gilded the waves of corn and tinted the snowy top of Elwand before I entered the city gates, near which I passed asses laden with snow, sure promise of cool sherbet and other creature comforts within.

150 miles.

The approach to Hamadan made a great impression on me. Luckily I descended upon it from the hills and did not crawl into it from the plain by the path as others have. Added to this it was a lovely day and the wheat was yet uncut. I thought it a rich landscape, such as Turner might have painted, bringing to life for the occasion to grace the scene the kings and warriors carved in imperishable rock at Besitoon and elsewhere on this once grand highway from Babylon to Persepolis.

Of the ancient city, however, its natural beauty alone remains. The modern town of Hamadan is one of the largest in Persia containing over 30,000 inhabitants. All the necessaries of life are extraordinarily cheap here. Dates and French sugar, Manchester goods, tea, and hardware are imported from Baghdad and dried grapes, almonds, skins, and carpets are exported. I was told that an Armenian lately came here from Mashad to buy cows and sheep for the Russians on the Afghan frontier, a queer story if true.

The sights of the town are three :—the tomb of Esther and Mordecai, who were, I was assured by the Jew who showed me around, husband and wife; the Gumbaz-i-Alabian, the remains of an ancient tomb with a florid internal decoration of the same character as that of the tomb near the Kutb Minar at Delhi; and a lion by the roadside, which was carved either before they had learnt or after they had forgotten the art of sculpture.

The mausoleum of Queen Esther is a poor little arched building, entered by a low door closed by a curious lock. It is odd to see a lock in Persia at all but this one, all of wood, with wooden tongue and tumblers and opened by the finger was particularly curious. Only the maker, the guardian of the tomb, knows how to open it. An arc-shaped cenotaph, of polished and very ancient-looking blackwood carved with Hebrew characters marks the spot where below the floor the queen rests and by its side is a similar cenotaph of smaller size for Mordecai. All around the walls are pasted little inscriptions in Hebrew.

From the hill outside the town, whence lately some skulls, pierced through the eyes and ears by nails, were dug, one sees that most of the houses are of two stories, and that the roofs are green with sprouting vegetation like those of the towns of Cashmere or the south-west coast of India. Nothing could be more significant of the difference between the climatic conditions of this locality and those of the greater part of Persia. Not that it is damp here.

A mountain stream tumbles through the middle of the town under bridges and over little waterfalls, and one of the main streets positively ends in a village green.

The success of the missionary here is confined as elsewhere in Persia to the conversion of Armenian Christians into Protestant Christians. One of these converts, when pressed to explain the distinction, stated that it chiefly consisted in this, that the former bathed in oil and the latter in water.

At Hamadan this little expedition ended, and paying off my two companions I started to ride through Kurdistan past Kermanshah to the Turkish frontier and thence to Baghdad. This road, though not so much frequented as it used to be, owing to the jealousies of the Turkish and Persian Governments, which have almost stopped the pilgrim traffic, is however in no sense unknown. The whole route is best described by Sir Robert Ker Porter, who has, however, hardly done justice to the beautiful plain of Minderabad, a huge pasture land, gay with gigantic hollyhocks and grazed over by innumerable cattle, sheep, and horses.

Halting at Kurdish camps, at Besitoun, and other places of interest in the country, some days elapse before the intervening 100 miles are passed and Kermanshah is reached, the chief town of these parts, where the British Government is represented by an agent, subordinate to the Minister at Teheran, Haji Ahsan, commonly called the Aga, whose reputation deserves to be even more widely spread than it is. Of great wealth, high character, and boundless hospitality, no Persian but the son of a rich merchant of Baghdad, this gentleman lives among his own people, to do good, caring nothing for the pleasures of the court, or the precarious advancement to be obtained by taking part in public affairs in Persia. Of several houses he inhabits one, the others being kept for guests of every rank and every nationality who pass this way. Outside his door is daily a greater crowd of petitioners than waits at that of official authority, and for every one is relief, redress, advice, or at least a kind word. Nightly 20 or 30 persons—some friends, some travellers, some poor of the town—dine on his carpets, besides his household, which includes a large number of devoted servants. Such influence and such a position as Haji Ahsan holds, I have not seen in the East, dissociated, as it is in his case, from official rank. His father was British Agent, and he hopes his son will be, and if, as he says, his secure position is due to the shadow of the Britith Government, that Government is no less fortunate in having so admirable a representative in so remote a spot.

A journey of some 60 miles of mostly stony hills, wherein the heat of a July sun was well nigh unbearable, brought me to the frontier where no traveller or caravan is allowed to proceed without an escort of two troopers. This would be pleasant enough for company's sake could they, as they rarely can, talk anything but Turki.

Kasr-i-Sheereen, the frontier station, is soon reached, and here a famous robber chief, Jawan Meer Khan, takes over the duty of escorting the traveller to a lonely watch-tower on the road to Khanakin, whence two Turkish troopers see him on to that town.

Just now Jawan Meer Khan robs nobody whose complaints might embarrass the Persian Government, which indeed pays him, I am told, 3,000 tomans, about £1,000, a year, for guarding the frontier. When my companion, a man of Kermanshah, and I got to his stronghold—he has a fort in good condition—he was lying on a stone seat covered with cushions, on the banks of the river, smoking his water-pipe in the moonlight and talking to his little son.

My companion slipped off and kissed his hand as he rose to receive us, a fine specimen of humanity, of unusual height and strength, aged perhaps 45, and covered, I am told, with the scars of wounds, though I did not notice them in the moonlight. On the way I had asked the Kermanshahi if Jawan Meer Khan was one of the grandees (buzurgan) of the country. "Certainly." "But" perversely, "is he not a robber?" "Certainly, but a great robber."

For many years this Kurdish chief has played Turks against Persians and Persians against Turks, robbing on both sides pretty impartially. In the Turko-Russian war he was commissioned to worry the Russian villages in Georgia, which he did, and then returned to his mountain fastness with the arms he had been supplied with—very good ones too. His men, said to be 200 in number, are exceedingly well mounted, and each is popularly said to be worth about 100 Persians, as most Kurds are. They are reckless riders, and the 12 miles between Kasr-i-Sheereen and the Turkish frontier were done in quicker time than any march I made in Persia, which here I leave behind me.

OOTACAMUND, J. D. R.
October 1885.

ITINERARY.

Kasveen to Mashaldar ... مشعلدار	Direction 180°, distance 5 miles, crossing the beds of two torrents, a well and two kanaats on the way. Village of 100 houses and 150 head of cattle. Close by is Pirsufian (پیرسوفیان).
Mashaldar to Farsian ... فارسیان	Direction 180°, distance 9 miles, pass small watch-tower, to the west of which is Kadimabad, afterwards another watch-tower and a hillock shaped like a sitting elephant. Houses 200, cattle 700 to 800. Hence Sultanabad in direction of 320°, Bulbulabad 40°.
Farsian to Ajurband ... آجوربند	Direction 180°, distance 11 miles, houses 50, cattle 60, inhabitants Turki. Hence Sakhsabad 160°.
Ajurband to Shaiantappa.	Direction 175°, distance 12½ miles, houses 50 to 60, inhabitants Turki. On the way pass Akhoora on the east, Husseinabad on west, and through Hakimabad.
Shaiantappa to Ardakh... ارداخ	Direction 220°, distance 17 miles, houses 300, cattle 200, sheep and goats 1,000.
Ardakh to Saidabad ...	Direction 180°, distance ¾ mile, houses 150, cattle 100, sheep, &c., 500. Within 3 or 4 miles of Saidabad are situated the following villages in the directions set against their names: Khurrumabad 245°, Javen 130°, Johareen 180°, Balaziyurt 200°, Deezan 100° east. In the last mentioned village camels can be obtained.
Saidabad to Juveen ... جوین	Direction 140°, distance 19¾ miles, leaving a large mound of earth on left and crossing a kanaat on the way. Houses 150, cattle 200, sheep, &c., 800.
Juveen to Maacheen ... معچین	Direction 180°, distance 22 miles, pass Mahomedabad and two large hillocks, pointing 240° and 250°, Idrabad, a kanaat, and the river Kharood.

Note.—The heights, as stated in the text, are only rough approximations from an aneroid, the statistics taken from observation and the statements of the villagers, the distances calculated by timing my horse's walk.

Maacheen to Zainabad ... زيناباد	Direction 180°, distance 24 miles, crossing affluent of Kharood, a kanaat and Khyrabad. Zainabad contains 200 houses. Inhabitants Turkis.
Zainabad to Ibrahimabad.	Direction 175°, distance 27¾ miles, houses 400, kanaats 1. Aneroid marks 4,500. About 3 miles hence, in direction of 170°, is Sagsábád (not Sagziabad), a large village of 500 houses, with head of cattle and sheep in proportion, and camels also.
Ibrahimabad to Ruak ... روك	Direction 180°, distance 35 miles, a slow ascent to 6,000 feet, uninterrupted as far as the orchards of Ruak or Rudak just visible from the plain, then a short descent and a brief ascent to the village. A watercourse runs down here to Ibrahimabad. Ruak contains 500 houses. Bullock-carts could ascend to this point without much difficulty.
Ruak to Alakaseer ... الاكسير	Direction 210°, distance 37 miles, along the west bank of Sagsabad river. Houses 300, cattle 200. Inhabitants Turkis. Road might be made fit for bullock-carts so far without much difficulty. Beasts of burden not obtainable at this or generally at any of the hill villages.
Alakaseer to Yeryan ... يريان	Direction 235°, distance 37½ miles, small hamlet of Alakaseer. Height 6,100.
Yeryan to Yalghoon ... يلغون	Direction 220°, distance 40½, along the Sagsabad river till joined by a hill torrent from the west.
Yalghoon to Chenara ... چناره	Direction 280°, distance 47 miles, past a ruined Eel village on the east, at first going 270°, but turning here to 280°, and thence up a long rising hill-side to Chenarah where the aneroid marks 7,300 feet. The track here would be difficult for wheels.

Chenara to Sumeinak ... سمينك	Direction 270°, distance 52½ miles, over various elevations to 8,000 feet, at Koh-i-Ramand, to Sumeinak (7,500 feet), a small Eel village of 20 houses. Road here in places very precipitous.
Sumeinak to Razzak ... رزك	Direction 270°, distance 56 miles, a poor village.
Razzak to Kulanjeen ... كلنجين	Direction 240° to Aliabad 60 miles and 270°, thence to Kulanjeen 67 miles. Before Aliabad, Chahbar, a small village, is visible in direction 160° from the path, and after Aliabad, a mere hamlet, a stream is crossed near a small Eel village, and yet another small Eel village and another stream are passed before Kulanjeen is reached. Kulanjeen has 700 houses, 500 head of cattle, and over 1,000 sheep, goats, &c. The Karaghan river flows west below it. A mile west of it on the river is Misrabad. Kulanjeen is 7,300 feet above the sea.
Kulanjeen to Meylakh ... ميلخ	Direction 200°, distance 68½ miles, down a fold in the hill-side to the valley of the Kharjistan river, which joins that of Karaghan between Kulanjeen and Misrabad. Meylakh has 50 houses.
Meylakh to Ooroo ... اورو	Direction 200°, distance 75 miles, passing a tomb on the west of the river. Village of 60 or 70 houses.
Ooroo to Haraeen ... هرائين	Direction 270°, distance 78 miles, elevation 8,000 feet, small hamlet.
Haraeen to Ainabad ... عيناباد	Direction 200°, distance 90 miles, across a branch of the Karaghan river, whence Goevak is situated 280° and Haraieen-i-bala 80°, both within half a mile, and Khoroosdarra 260° at a distance of 4 miles. Across a plain for 3 miles, then around a corner where the path overhangs a precipitous descent, next up the mountain side to 9,700 feet, whence after a descent of 1,000 feet, Shahbulagee is reached, a Turki hamlet of about a dozen houses. The road here is only just practicable for horses in many places. Ainabad is about 800 feet below this. I make the distance here from Kulanjeen 23 miles; the villagers say it is 22. Houses 120.

Ainabad to Shavand شوند	Direction 220°, distance 91½ miles, elevation 7,500. A poor and small village. Hence Sháhanjaveen is 180°, Káj 190°, Darjazeen 260°.
Shavand to Razeen رازين	Direction 220°, distance 96 miles; a small village with good gardens, vineyards and crops.
Razeen to Kurvah قروه	Direction 220°, distance 98 miles, passing Darjazeen on the right at a distance of 4 miles.
Kurvah to Sayan سايان	Direction 220°, distance 102 miles, village of about 100 houses. To the right of Sayan is Niyar.
Sayan to Harian حريان	Direction 200°, distance 105 miles.
Harian to Farmineen فارمنين	Direction 200°, distance 117 miles, passing on the left Dahla, Kalesa and Akela. Famineen, a large village of 750 houses, elevation 6,500 feet.
Farmineen to Janabad جاناباد	Direction 180°, distance 120 miles, passing Gulyuga Dagh or Hill. Hence 180° is Hamakasi, a village with a little fort on a hill.
Janabad to Nudah نداه	Direction 220°, distance 124 miles. Nudah is at the end of this second plain and at the foot of the second range of hills. On the way here Sarai, Mulagird on the right, and Sanah, Amirabad and Kishlah on the left are passed.
Nudah to Goorjoos كورجوس	Direction 210° to Eedali 6 miles and thence 180° to Kipchak, a small hamlet at an elevation of 6,900 feet, and Goorjoos 134 miles, a small village of about 30 houses at an elevation of 7,000 feet. Hence Bibikabad is 360° at a distance of 8 miles, and close to it is another village Yeseeralee.

Goorjoos to Surkhabad ... سرخاباد	Direction 220°, distance 144 miles, along grassy uncultivated hills to Aujabad, the smallest of hamlets, over a height of 7,500 feet, to Kirmis Kharaba, and thence to Surkhabad, a large and fertile village.
Surkhabad to Hamadan...	Distance 150 miles, past Mehrabad, Amirabad, Shuvareen to Hamadan.

www.ingramcontent.com/pod-product-compliance
Lightning Source LLC
Chambersburg PA
CBHW030710110426
42739CB00031B/1705